D1446861

ROOT SONG

ROOT SONG
Cid Corman

Potes & Poets Press Inc. Elmwood, Connecticut 1986.

Some of these poems have appeared - often in slightly different versions - in other collections published by THE ELIZABETH PRESS, ORIGIN, and some from little magazines. My thanks - of course - to all involved. And thanks also to The National Endowment of the Arts (Washington D.C.) for a grant (1973-74) that helped make this work possible.

for Robert Sanesi

I'm going ahead
to prepare the way.
Follow my silence
wherever it sing.

I.

I picked a
leaf up

it weighed
my vision

I knelt and
placed it

almost
where it was

I have come far to have found nothing
or to have found that what was found was
only to be lost, lost finally
in that absence whose trace is silence

Not myself
and not you
alone, but

each within
the other
moving out:

the tides of
earth and sky
shaping from

horizon
horizon,
orison

THE RITE

To say sky
as one says
water. To

pour it in-
to a cup
and hold it

at the lips
and drink. Of
it. And at

sundown to
drink it a-
gain as wine.

Dark morning
over the hills
cold flooding down
through pines

hands clap
invoking warmth
beating time to
a slow snow

The brink of the birdbath
where a bird bathed
sparkles

Each forgets what man is most:
nothing. And night becomes
a setting for devotions.

Snow that the wind today
drives horizontal will pass
in a moment into sun;

this we have seen, this we know -
but how moment holds the breath!
And then lets each one go.

At day's end
child asleep
in his arms

he steps light -
her bonnet
on his head

An old woman with
infant in her
arms or on her back

singing softly to
their swaying: today
loving tomorrow

THE GEOGRAPHER

What does that man
up on the jogging mule
saddlebags empty
coming down do

Each day's dawn he
picks up the thread and by
sundown again has
wound the hills home

THE CONTROL

We return to
silence, hearing
each other shake.

We nod as if
to admit the
hopelessness of

being here is
too obvious.
We learn to stop

trembling, almost
laughing, only
at times the flesh

leaps from itself,
as if beyond
weeping or hope

something in us
loved us and would
not wholly break.

THE PSALM

As nothing tempts flesh
to lift cry toward
silence and the sun,

my words twist shadows
of smoke. A tree spins,
the seasons unwind,

the rock ploughs dust, the
leaves begin to fret.
But strictly speaking

the dance is man's. O
more compassionate
than bread, be with me

god. Breathe in my song
what you are. And let
feet clasp the threshold.

Nobody forgets to die.
Some need to be reminded.

The hand you lifted from me
and placed upon your heart feels

how much I am moves in you,
how little an each each is.

The rain steadies
wisdom. After
the silences

are drummed out, from
the wild depths of
the heart the one

native hears truth.
He emerges
in to sun light.

What you are
I am. As if
to admit

the look in the
mirror of
the mirror. Not

nature to
be upheld - but
seen for what

it is: unseen
unless as
an edifice.

After the event
we know. Beyond the
dark fringe of the near

hill the crown beyond
of another height
given to sunlight.

To embrace
a tree - how
silly can
one get - yet

to want to
dance with it
the way the
wind's doing.

The hand I hold to the light
fills. What more do I offer you,
my love, than what the light gives?

Ask me when
I am dead
the meaning

of this. Then
each word will
answer you.

That old liar
Crow
Said only
Together together
Went on alone

ISE

A gate way
among
ancient pines

What man
goes through to
arrive

Drizzle. I'm going out soon
and so insist "I am".
Does it matter? Isnt rain

what I am wet by in it?
Like those webs in holly
spoiled as any diadem.

You sit there
at the bed's
edge and stare

at this man
trying to
sleep and you

say: Sleep, sleep...
But my dream
waits outside.

THE GRACE

Thank you for
whatever
it is - just
as it is

Ah - if we
could only
leave it at
that - at this.

I have come
it seems, to
meet you here

Say the word
and we part
together

II.

AREAS OF INTEREST

The telephone keeps ringing
the clouds hardly move

THE BALANCE

A sudden weightiness of
rain

received by the no sound of
earth.

Cicadas
'n' crickets

each of us
brings given

what no one
alone keeps

We have
nowhere to
get to

and so
much time to
arrive

Forever
was never
till now.

The way through the temple
never takes one to it -
but never to be there

is always to be here
under the bending pines
lending shadow shadow.

Hard to tell
sky from air
breath from word -
if one should.

A prince of great wealth
has abdicated,
lives in the realm of

a deep wood. Others,
like shadows, drift to
him. Silence offers

no word until he
lifts from the bud a
prayer for the sun.

Each of us each
moment nearer
death. As if we

slowly approached
the meaning of
the power of

breath. What other
hope is there for
our hopelessness?

So much more
than this is
this. And yet

how say it,
how expect
it to stand

beyond self
within this
emptiness?

SHARON

There is a green in dream called Spirit
to which the spirit returns. There
no oar lifts from what water one drop -

driven by heart - which fails to fall
glittering into the well of sky
amidst the pines and motion is

what moment is - reflection of that loss
absence trembling lifts and lifts and
empties of progression. Here who was

will be green within green absorbed
and breathing - the fire of the fire strained
immediately opening.

The train. I have said this before.
The train tracks the train tracks
successfully. Just the way things happen,

the way things are geared to happen.
The rail way. The sys tem.
We share what has been said before - again.

I could go out at dawn
and milk the grass of dew
and bring a cup to you

morning cool and clear,
but indolently dont.
I feel I have no use,

like smoke twisting nothing
around a strand of air.
I kneel - but as a root?

I yearn - but as a bough?
I die - but what flower
have I to offer night?

A GRACE FOR THE MEAL COMING

Thanks to the sun, the earth and the earthworm,
thanks to the worker in the field and hearts
through whom this food comes to this table, we
receive, as for the dead, these preparations.

From bamboo
flask into
bamboo cup

emptiness
the source of
drunkenness

THE TORTOISE

Always to want to
go back, to correct
an error, ease a

guilt, see how a friend
is doing. And yet
one doesnt, except

in memory, in
dreams. The land remains
desolate. Always

the feeling is of
terrible slowness
overtaking haste.

THE DESK

a god's head for a paperweight
and nothing to write

the large window open upon
an inner garden

harbored from heat
and the swamping dust of July

a dachshund romps among roses
and yaps at a yawn

the edge of the sky above the wall
the laurel tree tipping it in

it is hard to be anywhere once
and twice is a dream

What's the rush?
But no one
wants to wait.

This year's fruit
tastes only
slowly sweet.

A red
thread

on the no
stage

On the swept pond
snow sets
out

In the hills
for a few days -
couldnt write

Gone further found
less - maybe
you know the place

Slow to be
to be here:
rock occurs

Two pairs of black dragonflies
escort me as far as the gate
these mornings, as if I didnt
know where it was they are I'd be

The cow
belongs
to the good
green grass

crops close
but does
not bruise or
devour

Bell sound
bell silence

Who listens
listened

Heaven's net
cast so far -
not one star
escapes it

III.

High over
river
kite

Dont let go
and yet
go.

THE PUZZLE

At night snow
falling - how
each

piece always
fits into
place.

Slow motion
catastrophes
of cloud -

as if
we were seeing
destiny

played out in
the large terms of
nothing.

The rain comes
and the rain
goes. It seems

familiar.
Like something
we might know.

PAGODA

To the four
belled corners
seven eaves

hundreds and
hundreds of
swallows bring

hunger back
to the young
awaiting.

What in hell
do we think
we're doing

What am I -
to be clear -
up to here?

The Spirit
binds us and
releases

us. I am
trying to
say no more

than that I'm
trying to
say no more.

What have we done
that we should die
or did we do

to live? How to
trace a shadow's
finger with it?

Man, between your legs
the flute Apollo
rages at and will

flay you for. But go,
man, go - and be gone
into another.

You are crying, love,
in your dream again
and I reach into

the darkness to touch
you towards quiet.
When you sleep, so'll I.

It is not enough
to die - or to live.
But to live and die

together - at once -
and in every
moment each breath gives.

Always on
the verge of
returning

only to
find out one
has gone on.

Music may seek
nothing but
overwhelms

as flame climbs flame
ivy wall
to attain

nothing. The end
of silence
is silence.

No measure -
crocus or
kiku -

for the day
whose dying
this is.

Sappho
knew
nothing

more
than what
the

heart's word
brought
her to:

Be-
lovèd
be

loved (she
sings) -
and is

her
cry ours
too?

Who steals the
fire from whom?
And whose are
these ashes?

The gate here
without a
fence like a

door without
a house, man
without sense.

Surely - they
say - there is
more to life

than death. What
"more" can there
be than death?

One star
points far
near

All the
darkness
here.

A red leaf
boats the
stream

Call it "The
Life" like
so

many things
the light
brings.

Suddenly
sky comes
over
me

as more than
I can
it can
breathe.

No tide no
tidings gulls
eye

crying the
cry upon
the

long swing back
to land and
land.

To see and
bending touch
water -

what it is -
when what is
is this.

Do you know
what it means
to know what

it means to
be with you,
dear? I do.

Later the
stick returns
to shore

not where I
found it and
not here.

So that the
snow comes to
rest upon

snow. As if
no and no
and no came

in the end
to this. This
final yes.

Rain has the wind blown
and the night away

Shadows at daybreak
recall our journey.

Cid Corman

POTES & POETS PUBLICATIONS

Miekal And, Samsara Congeries, book 7
Bruce Andrews, Excommunicate
Bruce Andrews, from Shut Up
Todd Baron, dark as a hat
Lee Bartlett, Red Scare
Beau Beausoleil, in case / this way two things fell
Charles Bernstein, Amblyopia
Charles Bernstein, disfrutes
Clark Coolidge, A Geology
Cid Corman, Essay on Poetry
Tina Darragh, Exposed Faces
Alan Davies, a an av es
Alan Davies, Mnemonotechnics
Jean T Day, Unrest
Theodore Enslin, Meditations on Varied Grounds
Theodore Enslin, September's Bonfire
Peter Ganick, Two Space Six
Janet Hunter, in the absence of alphabets
P Inman, backbite
P Inman, waver
Jackson MacLow, Prose & Verse from the Early 80's
Barbara Moraff, Learning to Move
Janette Orr, The Balcony of Escape
Keith Rahmings, Printouts
Dan Raphael, Oops Gotta Go
Dan Raphael, The Matter What Is
Dan Raphael, Zone du Jour
Maria Richard, Secondary Image; Whisper Omega
Laurie Schneider, Pieces of Two
Ron Silliman, B A R T
Ron Silliman, from Paradise
James Sherry, Lazy Sonnets
Pete Spence, Almanak
Pete Spence, Elaborate at the Outline
Diane Ward, Being Another / Locating in the World
Craig Watson, The Asks
Hannah Weiner, Nijole's House

Potes & Poets Press Inc.
181 Edgemont Avenue
Elmwood, Connecticut 06110